A
Merry
Little
Christmas

A Merry Little Christmas

A Miniature Sleigh Full of Small Treats & Tiny Treasures

DIANA DUNKLEY

A LARK/CHAPELLE BOOK

A Division of Sterling Publishing Co., Inc.
New York

A Lark/Chapelle Book

Chapelle, Ltd., Inc.
P.O. Box 9255, Ogden, UT 84409
(801) 621-2777 • (801) 621-2788 Fax
e-mail: chapelle@chapelleltd.com
Web site: www.chapelleltd.com

Library of Congress Cataloging-in-Publication Data

Dunkley, Diana.
    A merry little Christmas: a miniature sleigh full of small treats
& tiny treasures / Diana Dunkley.
        p. cm.
    ISBN 1-57990-988-4 (pbk.)
1. Christmas decorations. 2. Handicraft. 3. Miniature craft. I. Title.

    TT900.C4D86 2006
    745.594'12-dc22

                                                    2006044733

10 9 8 7 6 5 4 3 2 1

First Edition

Published by Lark Books, A Division of
Sterling Publishing Co., Inc.
387 Park Avenue South, New York, N.Y. 10016

© 2006, Diana Dunkley

Distributed in Canada by Sterling Publishing,
c/o Canadian Manda Group, 165 Dufferin Street
Toronto, Ontario, Canada M6K 3H6

Distributed in the United Kingdom by GMC Distribution Services,
Castle Place, 166 High Street, Lewes, East Sussex, England BN7 1XU

Distributed in Australia by Capricorn Link (Australia) Pty Ltd.,
P.O. Box 704, Windsor, NSW 2756 Australia

Manufactured in China

ISBN 13: 978-1-57990-988-8
ISBN 10: 1-57990-988-4

For information about custom editions, special sales, premium and corporate
purchases, please contact Sterling Special Sales Department at 800-805-5489
or specialsales@sterlingpub.com.

Contents

Preface

IT was always an exciting day when my mother pulled out the Christmas boxes. There were only a few, but what treasures lay inside! My sisters and I would take turns pulling out the holiday decorations. We'd clap our hands and jump up and down with excitement as my father brought in the tree. Mother would cover it with a beautiful homemade tree skirt and then we'd start trimming it with colored balls and handmade ornaments we'd collected over the years.

The final touch was the tinsel. Mother insisted that we hang just a few strands at a time and that we cover every branch. Then the stockings—also handmade—were hung around the fireplace and the presents were brought in and arranged under the tree. It was a day of magic for a little girl.

A wonderful way for us to recapture that enchanted feeling we had as children is through the magic of miniatures. I remember the year when my father did exactly that. He decided that, after raising eight daughters, he'd had enough with dolls, dresses, tea sets, makeup, and high heels. So he bought himself a miniature train set, complete with a little sack of coal and an engine that blew real smoke. He spent hours setting it up under the tree and spent even more time watching it chug around the track. We spent hours just watching him. It was one of the rare times that I remember my father playing.

Christmas is the time of year when we let our inner child experience magic and wonder. This is the time of year when we create entire worlds in miniature. In doing so, we transport ourselves to imaginary settings, places where ice skaters twirl on glassy mirrored ponds, Santa Claus congregates with his elves, and the story of the first Christmas is recaptured in humble wooden crèches.

Enjoy the magic of miniatures by taking some time each year to add little treasures to your own home. This book is filled with beautiful things to create and Christmas traditions to begin, which will bring merriment and love to all those with whom you share the holidays. I invite you into these pages to discover new ideas to add to your own Christmas boxes. As you look and read, think of ways to make a project your own through colors, textures, and materials that appeal to you. Trust your instincts and the end results will be personal and magical.

Creating a Christmas in miniature is a joyful endeavor for me. I hope I can share that joy with you and that you, in turn, will share it with those you love. Here's to a magical, creative, and merry little Christmas.

Dana Dunkley

Christmas is
for children

Take a few moments to see Christmas through the eyes of a child. This
time of year, the world becomes magical and beautiful, an absolute feast for
the imagination. Things that are normally forbidden—from late bedtimes to
abundant amounts of candy—are allowed, just for this special time. Whatever
you do to indulge children's sugarplum visions this Christmas, we guarantee
that you will enjoy the experience of watching the magic unfold.

A Children's Table

Imagine, if you were a child, the delight of finding a fancy table laid out just for you, with plates, tea service, and silverware the right size for little hands. Such miniature treasures are sure to entertain children for hours.

For the dinner place setting, a bread-and-butter plate works perfectly, along with things like a miniature tea set, tiny salt spoons, and small champagne glasses. Add special touches usually reserved for adults at fancy dinner parties. Sparkling garlands, pretty napkin rings, personal nosegays, and decorative place cards make the table even more festive and special.

"It is good to be a child sometimes and never better than at Christmas, when its mighty founder was a child himself."
~ Charles Dickens

Child-Sized Berry Garland

Use this miniature berry garland to trim a children's table. It's lovely entwined around a silver tea set.

WHAT YOU NEED

26-gauge wire (16")
Craft scissors
Florist tape
Miniature lily of the valley (1 bunch)
Various jeweled berry sprays (3 stems)
Wire cutters

WHAT YOU DO

1. Using wire cutters, snip small lengths of berries and leaves from the major stem, leaving a 2"–3" stem on each one.

2. Cut ten pieces from florist tape to 8"–10" long. This makes it easier to handle.

3. Using florist tape, begin at one end of the wire and wrap the stems of berries together with the lily of the valley onto the wire, alternating until the entire piece is covered. Be certain to stretch the florist tape tightly while wrapping the stems.

MINIATURE GIFT BOXES PLACED AT EACH SETTING OR PILED UPON A SILVER PLATTER ADD TO THE GLAMOROUS LOOK OF THE CHILD'S DINNER TABLE. PLACE A LITTLE TREAT OR GIFT INSIDE, WRAP WITH WIDE SATIN RIBBON, THEN USE A NARROW RIBBON THREADED THROUGH A PEARL BEAD TO TIE THE WIDE RIBBON INTO A BOW TIE.

Miniature Nosegay

A miniature nosegay set at each child's plate says, "You're special." Place a corsage pin in each and let the children wear them throughout the party.

WHAT YOU NEED
½"-wide ribbon (16")
Fabric scissors
Florist tape
Jeweled berries (3 stems)
Vintage flower with stem

WHAT YOU DO

1. Arrange the berries and vintage flower in a small bouquet and wrap about 8" of florist tape around the stems.

2. Tie the ribbon around the base of the bouquet and trim ends to desired length.

CREATE YOUR OWN MINIATURE TOUCHES TO MATCH THE DECOR OF THE TABLE. HERE, I PLACED A SINGLE ROSE AND GREENS IN A SMALL CERAMIC CONTAINER. THESE ARE SMALL ENOUGH TO BE SET AT EACH PLACE SETTING. A SINGLE LONG-STEMMED MINIATURE ROSE LAID ACROSS A PLATE OR CLOTH IS ELEGANT, TOO.

Wreath Napkin Rings

These napkin rings are simple to make and simply beautiful. They add a festive adult elegance to a child's table.

WHAT YOU NEED
Miniature berry wreath
Small glass grapes
Tiny rosebud

WHAT YOU DO

1. Wrap the stems of the glass grapes around the wreath. Using the wire stem of the rosebud, further secure the grapes around the wreath.

2. Arrange the grapes and rosebud as desired.

Charmed Napkin Ring

This napkin ring begins with a key chain and ends with a tiny charm. You can personalize the rings by finding just the right charm for each young guest.

WHAT YOU NEED
1 ½" split key ring
26-gauge wire
Charm
Large pink beads
Small silver beads
Wire cutters

WHAT YOU DO

1. Cut a piece from wire to 30" long. Slip wire on key ring where keys would go. Wrap wire around ring two times to secure.

2. Thread beads onto the wire in a silver-pink-silver sequence. Wrap the wire tightly around the ring, making certain pink beads are along top of ring and silver beads are on the sides. Repeat this step until ring is completely covered with beads.

3. Slip end of wire through the O-ring of the charm.

4. Wrap excess wire around beads two or three times to secure.

WHAT YOU DO (FOR CAKES)

1. Bake cake according to package directions in a 9" x 13" pan. Cool, then cut into nine individual cakes. Position each cake on foam-core board.

2. Frost each cake with butter cream icing.

3. Knead chocolate fondant and roll out to ¼" thick. Cut into nine 9" x 10" pieces.

4. For each cake, gently wrap a square of fondant around a rolling pin to pick it up. Position it on the cake. Smooth and shape fondant with the palm of your hand. Trim off excess.

WHAT YOU DO (FOR BOWS)

1. Roll out pink fondant to ⅛" thick. Cut into nine 1" x 9" strips, eighteen 1" x 4" strips, and nine 1" x 3" strips.

2. Fold each 4" strip over to form a loop. Pinch and slightly dampen the ends with water to secure. Stand loops on their sides to dry.

3. Wrap a 3" strip around your finger to form the center of the bow. Brush ends with a damp pastry brush and adhere ends together.

4. Place ribbon strips on cake.

5. Insert ends of two loops into center loop to create a bow. Using a bit of water, adhere bow onto ribbon strip.

6. Place dots of icing around the base of the cake.

Present Cakes

Imagine a child's delight when you offer her an individual cake, wrapped up like a pretty present. Rolled fondant comes in several colors and is generally available at cake decorating stores.

WHAT YOU NEED

¼" x 3½" x 5" pieces of foam-core board (9)
Box of rolled chocolate fondant
Box of rolled pink fondant
Butter cream icing
Cake mix
Pastry brush
Rolling pin
Straight-edged kitchen knife
Water

CREATING CAKES WITH FONDANT

Fondant's smooth surface creates a professional look. Once you become familiar with it, you can use it to make all kinds of sweet little creations. Make an easy decorative look by simply piping dots or scrolls of butter cream icing onto a small fondant-covered cake, using a pastry bag and decorative tips.

You can also use the fondant itself to create decorations. Roll fondant out thinly and cut in strips to make lots of ribbon loops. Create flowers by cutting out petals, shaping them with your fingers to add dimension, and brushing a small amount of diluted food coloring in the centers. Add leaves brushed with green food coloring and small rolled pieces of yellow fondant to the centers to complete the flower look.

Place Cards

Children will be excited to find place settings reserved just for them, with elegant cards displaying their names.

WHAT YOU NEED

Decorative pin
Double-sided cardstock
Flower-shaped paper punch
Glass beads
Handmade paper
Patterned paper
Quick-drying craft glue
Spray bottle of water
Vellum

WHAT YOU DO

1. Cut cardstock to 3" square and fold in half.

2. Punch two flowers from patterned paper.

3. Place a dot of glue in the center of one flower, then place the second flower on top of it, staggering the petals. Pinch the tips of each petal to add dimension.

4. Cut a small strip from handmade paper and spray it with water. Remove a tiny piece and roll it into a ball. Glue the ball onto the center of the flower. Repeat five or six times.

5. While the glue is still wet, sprinkle glass beads into the center. Shake off excess.

6. Tear two small leaves from handmade paper and spray with water. Wrinkle each leaf, then smooth out and pinch the tips of the leaves. Glue them to the back side of the flower.

7. Print the name of guest on the vellum. Tear around the name, leaving enough room at the beginning to attach it underneath the flower. Use a decorative pin to hold vellum in place.

JUST AS YOU CAN SET A TABLE FOR YOUR CHILD, YOUR CHILD CAN SET A TABLE FOR HER DOLLS FOR A HOLIDAY TEA PARTY. THE CHARMING DISPLAY CAN REMAIN PART OF YOUR OWN HOLIDAY DECOR.

Projects for Little Hands

Children love to be busy, and at Christmas, there are lots of things they can make. Take a few minutes to organize a project for young hands.

So many projects can be made using simple items like newspaper, scraps of decorative paper, stickers, and buttons. Help children make little cards to send to family and friends by folding pieces of cardstock in half and letting them embellish as they please with stamps and stickers. To make simple ornaments, have children cut Christmas shapes out of paper. Decorate with glitter, stickers, adhesive jewels, and buttons. Punch a hole at the top and tie a pretty ribbon to hang the ornament on the tree.

Children can even make their own wrapping paper for the gifts they give to friends and family members. Simply roll out sheets of butcher paper and let children go wild with markers, Christmas stamps, and red and green ink pads. This paper is guaranteed to have more personality than any you'll find in a store.

Newspaper Star Ornament

This fun project is an easy way for kids to show their creativity. Let them go crazy and decorate their rooms, windows, or a small Christmas tree.

Braid (12" for each side of stars)
Craft scissors
Jewels (4–5 for each side of stars)
Newspaper
Quick-drying craft glue

WHAT YOU DO

1. Cut out 2" stars from newspaper.

2. Glue two stars together to give strength to newspaper.

3. Glue the braid around the outside edge of the star.

4. Glue on jewels. Repeat on remaining side, if desired.

A QUICK AND EASY PROJECT FOR KIDS IS TO HAVE THEM WRITE THEIR NAMES ON GLASS ORNAMENTS, USING METALLIC MARKERS. THEY WILL LOVE HAVING THEIR NAMES HANGING ON THE TREE.

Beaded Star

Little ones will be enchanted by these shiny stars that they can help make.

WHAT YOU NEED

Clear glass beads
Cord
Craft scissors
Double-sided adhesive sheets
Embellishments such as ribbon, beads, icicles, hearts, flowers, or leaves
Patterned paper
Quick-drying craft glue
Wooden stars of different sizes (3)

WHAT YOU DO

1. Trace around wooden stars on patterned paper and adhesive sheets. Cut inside the tracing line.

2. Glue patterned paper onto the star. Peel off one side of the adhesive sheet's paper backing and place over patterned-paper side of the wooden star. Peel off the other side of paper backing.

3. Place glass beads in a dish and place wooden star on the beads, pressing to apply beads.

4. Glue cord around the edges of the star, leaving about 6" at the top of the star to tie knots and make a loop.

5. Add embellishments as desired.

Christmas Tree Card

Tiny buttons add homespun charm to this card.

WHAT YOU NEED

1" x 5" green tulle
2½" x 6" parchment paper
Alphabet stamps
Beige embroidery floss
Brown ink pad
Craft scissors
Green textured cardstock (1 sheet)
Hole punch
Needle
Quick-drying craft glue
Tiny buttons (6)
Pattern (page 106)

WHAT YOU DO

1. Fold parchment paper in half to form a card.

2. Trace card tree pattern onto green cardstock. Cut out.

3. Rub inside and edges of card and tree on brown ink pad.

4. Stamp "Merry Christmas" onto the front of the card.

5. Stitch buttons onto the tree, using embroidery floss. Glue the tree onto the front.

6. Cut a piece from green cardstock to 2" x 5½". Fold in half. Glue inside the card.

7. Punch two holes through the front of the card. Thread ends of tulle through the front and tie in a bow.

MAKING CARDS IS EASY WITH THE RIGHT MATERIALS. GIVE CHILDREN DECORATIVE CARDSTOCK, CHRISTMAS STICKERS, RIBBONS, TRIMS, AND KID-FRIENDLY SCISSORS, AND LET THEIR IMAGINATIONS GO TO WORK. YOU WILL BE IMPRESSED WITH THEIR CREATIVITY.

Pop-Up Christmas Card

This is a good project for you and your kids to create together. Let them do the folding and decorating while you measure and cut.

WHAT YOU NEED

Craft knife

Craft scissors

Double-sided patterned cardstock

Holiday sticker sheet, such as snowmen and snowflakes

Quick-drying craft glue

Red patterned paper

Red pom-pom

WHAT YOU DO

1. Cut a cover 3" x 7" from cardstock. Fold in half.

2. Cut pieces from red paper for the inside to 2¾" x 6¾", 2½" x 3", 1½" x 2½", and 1" x 2". Fold each of these pieces in half. With craft knife, cut a slit into the center of each piece's fold to ½" wide and 1½" deep (Diagram 1). Pop the slit out in the opposite direction of the fold (Diagram 2).

3. Place red pieces of paper inside the card, staggering each piece so the slits are not directly in front of each other. Glue each one onto the back of the one in front of it.

4. Attach snowmen stickers and snowflakes as shown in photo.

5. Cut a piece from cardstock to ½" x 2½" and fold it in half. Type the words "You're 'Snow' Cute! Merry Christmas" and glue it onto the front pop-up.

6. Glue the red pom-pom onto the front snowman.

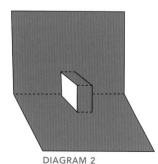

DIAGRAM 1

DIAGRAM 2

Mitten Tags

Homemade tags make a
child's gift even more special.

WHAT YOU NEED

⅛"-wide green ribbon (6")
Computer
Craft scissors
Fabric scissors
Green checkered paper
Printer
Quick-drying craft glue
Red cardstock
Round red brad
White cardstock
White felt
Green ink pad
Patterns (page 106)

WHAT YOU DO

1. Trace mitten top pattern onto green checkered paper twice and cut out.

2. Trace cuff pattern onto white felt and cut out.

3. Trace whole mitten pattern onto red cardstock twice and cut out.

4. Glue green checkered paper and white felt onto red cardstock, placing the felt below the checkered paper.

5. Attach the brad to the felt, going through both mittens.

6. Tie one end of the ribbon around the brad on the front and the other end onto the back of the brad.

7. Print "To.." and "From.." onto white cardstock. Cut around and lightly brush the edges across the top of the green ink pad. Glue onto the top of each mitten.

HELP KIDS MAKE ALL KINDS OF MINI POP-UP CARDS, USING REDUCED COLOR-COPIED FAMILY PHOTOS AND DIFFERENT PAPER SHAPES. JUST LEAVE EXTRA SPACE IN THE FOREGROUND FOR THE PHOTO, AND ADHERE DESIRED CUTOUTS TO PAPER FOLDS.

A Child's World

A child's world at Christmas is filled with imagination. Treat your family to a special outing during the holidays and observe the world at a child's pace. When you take time to linger at displays, you will find that you notice more details and that you simply enjoy the Christmas atmosphere even more.

Seek out Christmas miniatures, trains, dolls, and dollhouses in your area. Museums, Christmas festivals, and trade fairs will often have special collections on exhibit. Stop to enjoy displays at toy stores, at the mall, and inside store windows. Slow down to a relaxed pace, and best of all, enjoy watching your children as they are filled with the wonder of miniatures.

Storefront Displays

Behold a child's awe as she gazes at vignettes full of miniature people in a make-believe city. Children's vibrant imaginations bring these scenes to life; they can almost picture the figures twirling on a tiny pond and shouting Christmas greetings to each other.

Department stores go all out for Christmas, dressing windows in elaborate holiday scenes. Make a new tradition this year of going downtown to visit the many window displays and to simply see the city at Christmas. Sip hot chocolate, nibble on roasted chestnuts from a street vendor, and listen to sleigh bells on horse-drawn carriages as you and your children gaze at the wondrous scenes.

"Our hearts grow tender with childhood memories and love of kindred, and we are better throughout the year for having, in spirit, become a child again at Christmas-time."

~ Laura Ingalls Wilder

Decorated Dollhouses

If your child has a dollhouse, decorating it for Christmas with her can become a delightful tradition that you share together. Create holiday decor with tiny trees, presents, or stockings. Each year, add a new item, whether you find it at a store or create it yourself.

Don't forget the door. A tiny wreath on the front entry is a realistic detail that adds a charming touch. Try making wreaths with rags, twine, raffia, or vines. Finish with a bow, silk flowers, or jewels. Tiny wreaths sold as ornaments can be found ready to hang.

"Were I a philosopher, I should write a philosophy of toys, showing that nothing else in life need to be taken seriously, and that Christmas Day in the company of children is one of the few occasions on which men become entirely alive."

~ Robert Lynd

Though an exquisite dollhouse is a wonderful setting for displaying miniature scenes, it isn't necessary. Making a dollhouse room inside a box is a great project that both you and your child can enjoy. Decorate the exterior of the box any way you wish, then create an entire room on the inside. Make windows by cutting out panels from the box and adhering sections of plastic sheeting, cut to size, over the open area. Furnish the interior with leftover pieces of wallpaper and scraps of fabric for curtains and carpets. Then arrange a holiday scene with furniture, dolls, and Christmas decor.

Animal Characters

Miniature animals portraying holiday scenes are especially charming. Whether depicting a quiet evening around the fire, a noisy dinner with relatives, or a lively party with plenty of song and dance, they bring an extra dose of Christmas cheer.

Tiny stuffed dogs, cats, or bears can be purchased at most toy stores and dressed in Christmas finery with a few scraps of fabric, trim, a needle, and thread. This can be a lovely surprise for your little ones on Christmas morning.

When creating Christmas vignettes, draw on holiday traditions as inspiration. You might portray a turkey dinner,

the bustle of Christmas morning, children hanging stockings, a kiss under the mistletoe, or the decorating of the tree.

A cozy miniature scene depicting Grandpa reading "The Night Before Christmas" captures the eager anticipation of little ones as they await the arrival of Santa Claus. Thoughtful details, like the stockings hanging from the mantel and pajamas on the young ones, complete the scene.

Merry Little christmas trees

Christmas just isn't Christmas without a tree. It is one of our favorite holiday traditions. Whether you hang the branches with scaled-down items or make mini evergreens to place throughout your home, trees will always capture the magic of miniatures.

Miniature Christmas Trees

Miniature trees are a great way to bring Christmas cheer into every room of the house. Their small size means you can decorate them quickly, so you will have more time for friends and family.

These pages give ideas for all kinds of trees, from synthetic glam to natural and woodsy. You are sure to find one to fit your style. Try placing them on tables, sideboards, dressers, or mantels. Anywhere you put them, you will find added holiday cheer.

"As well might we dance without music, or attempt to write a poem without rhythm, as to keep Christmas without a Christmas tree."

~ Weekly Press, 1877

Retro Tinsel Tree

Bring back memories from the glamorous fifties with this glitzy tabletop tinsel tree.

WHAT YOU NEED

⅛" drill bit and drill

1"-diameter dowel

6"-square container

Band saw

Floral foam

Hot-glue gun and glue sticks

Quick-drying craft glue

Silver tinsel garland

Spray insulating foam

Suspended-ceiling wire

White tinsel or shredded glass

Wire cutters

WHAT YOU DO

1. Using the band saw, cut dowel to 24" long.

2. Hot-glue floral foam into container. Place dowel in floral foam, making certain it is straight. Use insulating foam to fill in around the floral foam and dowel. Leave 2" at top of container, as the insulating foam will expand. Let dry overnight.

3. Drill four holes around the dowel, starting 4" from the bottom. Make certain to stagger holes so the wires inserted later will not hit each other. Measure up 3" for next set of four holes. Drill three more sets of holes, with each set spaced 3" apart. Drill the last two sets of holes 2" apart. (You should have a total of seven sets of holes.) Drill a hole into the top of the dowel.

4. Cut four pieces from wire to each length: 7", 3", and 2". Cut eight pieces from wire to 5" and eight pieces to 6". Cut a piece from wire to 3" for the top hole.

5. Starting at the bottom holes and using the longest wire pieces, apply hot glue to the end of the wire and insert into the holes. Hot-glue the next longest wire pieces into the next holes. Continue this way all the way up the dowel. Insert the 3" wire into the top hole.

6. Place a line of glue along the top of one piece of wire. Wrap tinsel garland around wire, starting from the dowel and working out. Repeat until all wire pieces are covered. Apply glue to dowel, then wrap with tinsel garland until dowel is covered.

7. To cover insulating foam, spread quick-drying craft glue over entire area and sprinkle with white tinsel.

SEARCH FOR SHINY MINIATURE RETRO ORNAMENTS TO PLACE ON YOUR TREE. GLASS BALLS IN SHADES OF METALLIC PINK AND ICE BLUE OR PAINTED GLASS FIGURINES WORK BEAUTIFULLY. YOU MIGHT HAVE OLD ORNAMENTS FROM YEARS AGO, OR YOU CAN FIND SOME AT A SECONDHAND STORE.

Tin Tree

*Ribbon and roses add a soft,
romantic feel to a charming tin tree.*

WHAT YOU NEED

½"-wide sheer ribbon
Fabric scissors
Florist tape
Hot-glue gun and glue sticks
Small berry sprays (2 per branch)
Small silk rosebud sprays with leaves
   (1 per branch)
Tin or metal tree with branches for candles
Wire cutters

WHAT YOU DO

1. Using wire cutters, cut off 1" pieces of stem
   with one rosebud and one leaf. *Note: Leaf can be
   applied separately if including it makes the stem too long.*

2. Cut off berries, leaving 1" and 3" stems.

3. Cut ribbon into 8" pieces, enough for
   each branch.

4. Cut three 8" strips of florist tape.

5. Cluster the two berries, bud, and
   leaf together.

6. Loop one-half of the ribbon, leaving one
   long end. Fold the long end back so that it
   lies underneath the loop. Place the berry-bud
   cluster on top of the ribbon and wrap with
   florist tape. Continue wrapping until stems
   are completely covered with tape.

7. Place the cluster on the tip of a branch and
   glue into place.

8. Repeat until all the branches are decorated.

Topiary Tree

*This grapevine tree lends a European
country chic to your home.*

WHAT YOU NEED

½"-wide ribbon

2 types berries

2 types Christmas greens

10"-square plastic foam, 1" shorter in
   height than the box

10"-square wooden box

26-gauge green wire

Bird

Curly willow or other twigs

Grapevine garland (32")

Hot-glue gun and glue sticks

Miniature ivy

Moss

Spray insulating foam

Suspended-ceiling wire

Wire cutters

WHAT YOU DO

1. Soak grapevine garland in water overnight so
   it is pliable.

2. Work ceiling wire through the grapevine garland
   from one end to the other. Trim off excess wire.

3. Find the center of the grapevine and bend it
   into the shape of a tree. *Note: The tree's trunk must
   be 4" long. Wire the two pieces for the trunk together
   with floral wire.*

4. Using floral wire, secure curly willow around
   the grapevine tree.

5. Glue plastic foam into box. Insert tree into foam.
   Spray insulating foam on top of the plastic foam.

6. Place moss around the base of the tree, making
   certain to cover the foam completely.

7. Hot-glue berries, ivy, and greens onto the tree
   as desired.

8. Arrange greens and berries at the bottom of the
   tree. Hot-glue bird onto arrangement.

9. Tie ribbon in a bow at the center of the length of
   ribbon and glue onto the top of tree, leaving long
   ends to wind around tree to bottom. Work ribbon
   into the arrangement at the bottom of the tree,
   leaving ends long enough to hang over the box.

Clay Pot Tree

Nesting flowerpots are perfect for stacking into a little "tree."

WHAT YOU NEED

Bead garland
Beaded tinsel garland
Hot-glue gun and glue sticks
Silver nesting clay pots (5)
Tiny stars and icicles

WHAT YOU DO

1. Starting at the bottom, from large to small, hot-glue pots onto top of each other.

2. Wrap tinsel garland and beads around the tree, gluing as you go.

3. Glue a star onto the top.

4. Tie tiny stars and icicles onto the tinsel garland.

"Christmas is the season for kindling the fire of hospitality in the hall, the genial flame of charity in the heart."

~Washington Irving

Tiny Twig Trees

*These tiny trees bring nature indoors
and add a soft sparkle with glitter
and berries.*

WHAT YOU NEED

Berry spray
Craft scissors
Flower spray
Glitter branch spray
Hot-glue gun and glue sticks
Twigs

WHAT YOU DO

1. For the large tree, cut a 12" straight twig for center and about fifty 6" twigs for branches. For the small tree, use an 8" straight twig for center and about 25 twigs for branches.

2. Beginning at the bottom, hot-glue the twigs around the base of the tree. Hold each branch in place until secure. Continue to the top, using shorter twigs for each consecutive layer.

3. Cut off berries and leaves from berry spray. Hot-glue flowers, berries, and leaves along the trunk of the twig tree to cover the glue. Arrange as desired.

4. Cut glitter spray into single branches and hot-glue them onto different areas of the trunk.

Memory Tree

This miniature wire tree is perfect for displaying old photos and cards. No need to worry about fragile keepsakes because these photos and cards have been reduced and copied.

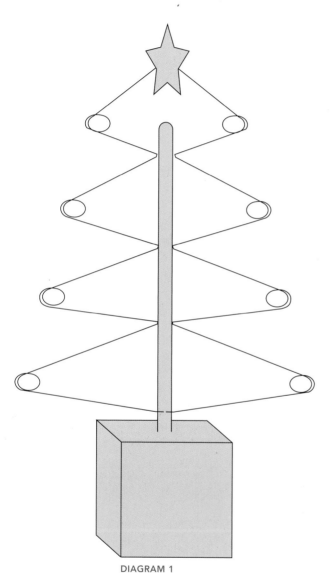

DIAGRAM 1

WHAT YOU NEED

¹⁄₁₆" **drill bit and drill**

¼"**-diameter dowel**

1" **sponge brush**

2" **wooden block**

5½"**-long spindle**

9**-gauge wire**

26**-gauge wire**

Silver acrylic paint

White crackle paint

Drill bit the size of end of spindle

Hot-glue gun and glue sticks

Metal embellishments

Reduced color-copied old photographs and cards

Small decorative star

Wire cutters

Wood glue

Sandpaper

WHAT YOU DO

1. Drill a hole in the center of the block with spindle-sized drill bit. Using the sponge brush, paint the block silver. Let paint dry.

2. Paint the spindle with the white crackle paint. Let paint dry.

3. Glue the spindle into the block.

4. Cut two 26"-long pieces of wire. Starting at top of tree, measure 1" down from the end of the wire and wrap wire around the dowel two times at measured area. Move down 1¼" from the loop and wrap wire around dowel two times in the opposite direction of the first loop. Continue down the wire this way, adding ½" between loops for every bough of tree until you have completed four loops (Diagram 1). Repeat with the remaining piece of wire.

5. Using ¹⁄₁₆" drill bit, drill a small hole through the spindle 1" from the bottom. Hot-glue wire ends into hole.

6. Using the sponge brush, paint wire white. Let paint dry. Rough up with sandpaper.

7. Hot-glue decorative star onto the top of the tree.

8. Slip cards and photos into loops on tree to display.

THEME TREES

Creating miniature trees is easy with prepurchased trees and a bit of creativity. Choose a theme, then search for ornaments within that theme or create your own decorations.

Make a bejeweled tree with glittering silver and gold ornaments and a pearl garland. A natural tree can be created with small pinecones and acorns from your yard. Drape it with a mini fruit garland made from dried slices of crabapples and kumquats to simulate apples and oranges. A delicate, spare fir is perfect for an ethereal angel tree, embellished in wisps of lace. Just use your imagination—the possibilities are endless.

Tiny Treasures for the Tree

Part of the fun of decorating trees, large and small, is finding and creating miniature decorations to hang on the branches. On these pages, you will find ideas and projects for making tiny treasures for the tree, from frilly to metallic to natural.

A beautiful Christmas tree should not only dazzle from afar, but also be delightful upon closer inspection. Think about the hours you spent as a child beholding the miniature wonders on your family's tree, or about the festive atmosphere that you enjoy as an adult from a beautifully decorated tree. When you give time and attention to little details, the results are stunning from any viewpoint.

> "The tree was planted in the middle of a great round table, and towered high above their heads. It was brilliantly lighted by a multitude of little tapers; and everywhere sparkled and glittered with bright objects."
>
> ~Charles Dickens,
> "A Christmas Tree," 1850

Paper Cones

These cones, filled with miniature mints, a miniature candy cane, or stick candy, are wonderful treats to hang on the tree for little ones. They also make great party favors. (See page 52 for more cone ideas.)

WHAT YOU NEED

26-gauge wire

Craft scissors

Glass beads

Quick-drying craft glue

Scrapbook or decorative paper

Small hole punch

Trim

Pattern (page 106)

WHAT YOU DO

1. Trace cone pattern onto back side of paper. Cut out.

2. Roll into cone shape. Make certain top edges align where paper meets, then glue together. Glue trim around the top of cone. Punch two small holes $\frac{1}{16}$" from the top on opposite sides of cone. Position the holes so that the seam will be in the back when the handle is attached.

3. Cut a 3"-long piece of wire. Insert one end of wire into the hole. Twist the end with the long piece to secure. Thread beads onto the wire, leaving enough wire to insert into the hole and secure on opposite side. Twist to secure.

4. Cut a 1½"-long piece of wire. Fold in half, leaving a small eyehole at the end. Place a bead on the end of the wire. Apply glue to the wire. Slip it into the bottom point of the cone, pushing the bead through the bottom hole. Make certain wire is touching paper on the inside to secure.

51

PAPER CONE IDEAS

Small paper cones are easy to make or embellish. Splurge on some luxurious paper. Add texture with glitter and beads. For trim, try a boa, sequins, pom-poms, tinsel, or ribbons with beaded fringe.

Tailor the treat inside to the decor of the cone. Pastel taffy or meltaway candies are perfect for frilly pink cones. Gold-wrapped caramels suit gilded cones. Look for unusual colors of jellybeans and select two or three hues to complement a colorful cone.

Crochet Bear Ornaments

Small crocheted bears look whimsical displayed on Christmas greenery. To create your own collection of holiday bears, you don't need to spend time crocheting—simply purchase miniature teddy bears or plain bear ornaments and embellish them yourself. Sew on ribbons, tiny wire eyeglasses, hats, and scraps of fabric for scarves. Place the bears on tiny sleighs, or give them musical instruments. You can create a Christmas morning scene by adhering tiny boxes and toys to the bears' hands. Just use your imagination and see what wonderful creations result.

Pillow Ornaments

Hanging on the tree, these darling miniature pillows invite Christmas cheer.

WHAT YOU NEED

¾"-wide trim (7")
3½" x 4" piece of fabric
Adhesive interfacing
Cord with tassels
Fabric scissors
Iron
Needle and matching thread
Polyester stuffing
Sewing machine and
    matching thread
Wire words
Wired beads

WHAT YOU DO

1. Iron trim onto adhesive interfacing, then iron trim to right sides of fabric in desired area. Place right sides of fabric together. Make a loop with cord and place the cord ends at the top of the pillow. Sew sides together, making certain to attach cord as you sew. Leave a small opening at the bottom.

2. Turn the pillow right side out. Stuff pillow with polyester stuffing. Whip-stitch the opening closed.

3. Stitch the wire words onto the front of pillow. Place wired beads around the cord loop at top of pillow.

PILLOWS AND SACHETS

Once you know how to make a basic miniature pillow, you can begin playing around with different fabrics, colors, shapes, and trims. Try making several for the tree in complementary patterns and colors.

You can also use the pillow-making technique to create scented sachets. Instead of filling the cases with polyester stuffing, fill them with the aromas of Christmas. You can use prepurchased holiday potpourri, as long as the pieces are small enough to fit inside the mini sachets. Or, you can make your own. For a pine-scented sachet, mix four parts dried fir needles with one part dried rosemary, a few crumbled bay leaves, a bit of dried basil, and two parts coarse salt (this helps keep the fragrance longer). To make a citrus-spice scent, mix two parts chopped dried citrus peels with one part coarse salt. Add small amounts of ground cloves, ground cinnamon, and any other spices you wish until you achieve the desired aroma.

These mini scented sachets make wonderful gifts, ornaments for the tree, or decorations in a bowl on the table.

55

Stars and Hearts

Made of wire screen and embellished with gold and jewels, these glittering ornaments enhance this tree's metallic chic.

WHAT YOU NEED

Bag of assorted clear jewels
Craft scissors
Hot-glue gun and glue sticks
Marker
Narrow gold braid (15" per ornament)
Screen, new or old
Tiny glass beads
Patterns (page 107)

WHAT YOU DO

1. Trace heart and star patterns onto the screen with marker. Cut out.

2. Apply a thin line of glue along the edge of the star or heart. Dip quickly into a pile of beads. Shake off excess and pat beads softly so they adhere firmly. Repeat until edges of all ornaments are beaded.

3. Hot-glue jewels onto front and back of ornaments.

4. Thread each length of braid through the tip of each star ornament and the center of each heart, then tie onto the tree.

Wire Wreath

Try making wreaths out of both silver wire and copper wire. The metallic sheen of each goes well with a wrought-iron tree.

WHAT YOU NEED

½"-wide wire-edged ribbon (15")
16-gauge wire (100")
Bag of multicolored jewels in
    assorted sizes
Hot-glue gun and glue sticks
Wire cutters

WHAT YOU DO

1. Cut a 16" piece of wire. Set aside (this will be used later as vine ends).

2. Leaving 8" on the end of the remaining wire straight, begin making loops about 3" in diameter. Wrap wire around eight times, making each loop slightly irregular. After making the last loop, leave another 8" of wire straight. Trim excess wire. These 8" lengths of wire will also be vine ends.

3. Lay the 16" length of wire alongside the other vine ends at the top of the wreath. Wrap one of the 8" ends tightly around all the wire in the wreath and vine ends. Do this about five times.

4. Wrap the four wire ends around a pencil to curl.

5. Tie a bow around the top of the wreath with ribbon. Hot-glue one jewel in the center of the bow. Hot-glue jewels at random around top half of wreath.
    Note: Gluing the jewels back-to-back, with the wire in between, will better secure them.

Felt Stocking

This cute stocking can be decorated in any way imaginable. We give instructions for the polka dot one, but variations require only imagination.

WHAT YOU NEED

½" hole punch
Embroidery floss
Fabric adhesive
Fabric scissors
Green felt
Red felt
Ribbon with beaded fringe
Small bell
Pattern (page 107)

WHAT YOU DO

1. Cut two stockings from red felt as shown in photo at center above, using felt stocking pattern. Cut a cuff from green felt to fit.

2. Cut strips from green felt for the toe and heel. Punch out polka dots, using hole punch.

3. Using fabric adhesive, glue stockings together, leaving top open.

4. Glue cuff onto top of stocking. Glue toe and heel strips onto stocking. Glue felt polka dots onto stocking as desired.

5. Glue ribbon on the inside of top edge so that beaded fringe hangs over the edge.

6. Cut strip from felt to ¼" x 3" for loop hanger. Glue into place.

7. Thread floss through bell and tie onto loop.

MINI STOCKINGS

To make these fun and easy ornaments, use the felt stocking pattern on page 107 or your own pattern as a starting point and experiment with different fabrics and embellishments. Create a country look using old clean dishtowels or tablecloths, and embroider the stockings with names, designs, and Christmas sayings. Make fancy silk jester stockings by drawing a pattern with a curled toe and using silky, rich fabrics and trims. With a little creativity, you can create all kinds of styles.

Natural and Elegant Treasures

You can create a variety of elegant and natural ornaments using items that you might be able to find in your own yard. Small wreaths or balls made of twigs are a great place to start. Attach wired jewels onto a ball of natural vine and twigs. Try looping wired beads into a wreath and add sheer ribbon for a delicate, graceful look.

Search the floral department of a crafts store for tiny faux berries and other fruits, dried flowers and plants,

pinecones, acorns, gilded leaves, and more to create beautiful earthy treasures. Glue dried berries or pinecone cuttings onto plastic foam balls, or adhere tiny pinecones and acorns onto a small plastic foam wreath. Embellish with silk and ribbon, and any natural delights you may find.

A fragrant heart wreath is a beautiful item for the tree or to give away as a handmade gift. Make your own with wire and sprigs of lavender. The purple hue looks absolutely stunning among the green needles of a fir tree.

The *Best Things*
come in small packages

It is said that the best things come in small packages, and we agree. Miniature gifts can have a big impact, especially when cleverly presented in a small, creative container. This chapter is filled with ideas for little gifts in unique packages that will delight recipients of all ages.

Photographs make very thoughtful Christmas gifts and meaningful decorations. The second half of this chapter presents a collection of miniature frames and albums you can make to keep or to give. Just working on these projects will fill you with the spirit of the season.

Miniature Gifts

Small-scale presents, especially when made by hand, are always fun to give and receive. The gifts on these pages range from tiny doll kits to tic-tac-toe games to sweet treats.

Little containers, like tins, mini hatboxes, small cans, paper boxes, and clay pots, are a perfect way to present miniature gifts and in many cases can be the best part of the gift! Search the crafts store for plain, inexpensive containers. Then have fun adding simple embellishments or changing the look completely.

Small containers can be quickly and easily decorated. Try decoupaging decorative paper onto containers. For extra glam, coat the paper with glitter or tiny confetti before the decoupage medium dries, then give it an extra coat to seal it. You can glue pretty fabrics, ribbons, and trims to containers, using craft glue or fabric adhesive. Shroud an entire box, perhaps, in glittery sequins or gems. Just use your imagination, and you will end up with pretty little containers ready to be filled with all kinds of treasures and treats.

Tic-Tac-Toe Tin

This is a great gift for kids. The recipient can carry the tin in his or her pocket, ready for a quick game at a moment's notice.

WHAT YOU NEED

¼"-wide ribbon (½ yard)
Fabric scissors
Miniature hat ornaments (4)
Miniature mitten ornaments (4)
Quick-drying craft glue
Round magnets (8)
Ruler
Tiny round tin

WHAT YOU DO

1. Measure the lid, including the edge. Cut ribbon into four strips at the determined measurement.

2. Glue ribbon onto the lid of the tin, forming a tic-tac-toe board. Trim off excess.

3. Glue one ornament onto each magnet. Let dry, then place magnets inside of the tin.

A TINY CLAY POT IS A UNIQUE WAY TO GIVE A GIFT. DECOUPAGE PRETTY PAPER ONTO THE POT, THEN FILL WITH LITTLE PRESENTS WRAPPED IN COORDINATING GIFT WRAP.

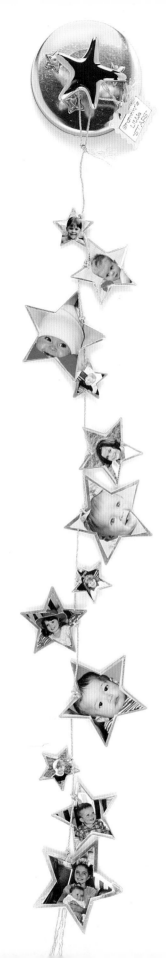

Photo Star Tin

*This darling tin holds a surprise inside:
upon opening, a string of photo-filled
tags appears.*

WHAT YOU NEED

1¹⁄₆₄" drill bit and drill
Package of metal-edged star tags
Quick-drying craft glue
Round tin
Silver cord (1 yard)
Star drawer pull

WHAT YOU DO

1. Drill a hole into the center of the lid.
   Screw the drawer pull into the lid.

2. Cut photos to fit inside each side of
   the star tags.

3. Tie the silver cord though each star
   tag's hole, leaving enough room for
   the stars to hang below each other.
   Repeat until all tags are hung.

4. Tie the top end of the cord around the
   drawer pull so that when the lid is
   lifted, all of the stars come out of the
   tin attached to the lid.

Favorite Things Tin

Take a few minutes to find miniature versions of your child's favorite things, such as bears, dolls, blocks, and books. She will be so pleased to receive this personalized present.

WHAT YOU NEED

¼"-wide sheer ribbon (8")
Brads (4)
Child's miniature favorite things
Decoupage medium
Flowers
Heart tag labeled with child's name
Patterned paper
Slide mount (available at scrapbook stores)
Tin box with lock and key

WHAT YOU DO

1. With the decoupage medium, adhere patterned paper onto the outside of the tin and inside the lid of the tin.

2. Cover the patterned paper with decoupage medium. Adhere flowers, the slide mount with "Favorite Things" written inside, the heart tag, and ribbon onto the top of the lid.

3. Place child's favorite items inside.

IF YOU CANNOT FIND A TIN BOX WITH A LOCK AND KEY, ANY CONTAINER WILL DO. THIS LITTLE CARDBOARD BOX, BEDECKED WITH A JEWEL AND A PAPER POINSETTIA, WORKS JUST AS WELL.

Clothespin Doll Kit

This kit provides all of the necessary materials for making simple, homespun dolls.

WHAT YOU NEED

¹⁄₁₆"-wide ribbon
Adhesive dots
Buttons
Decoupage medium
Fabric adhesive
Fabric squares or scraps (6)
Felt squares (6)
Marker
Packages of doll hair
Patterned paper
Pieces of lace
Pipe cleaners
Small elastics
Suitcase tin
Tag
Wooden clothespins (6)

WHAT YOU DO

1. With the decoupage medium, adhere patterned paper to the lid and outside of the tin.

2. Write "Clothespin Doll Kit" on the tag. Attach the tag with a bow around a clothespin. Add buttons with adhesive dots to the tag and tin.

3. Place elastics around clothespins, fabric squares, felt squares, pieces of lace, and ribbon. Place inside the tin.

4. Make one doll as a sample: **a.** Wrap pipe cleaners around the head to create arms. **b.** Using fabric adhesive, glue felt onto the trunk and arms for the shirt. **c.** Glue fabric onto shirt for the skirt. **d.** Glue lace under the skirt for a slip. **e.** Glue buttons to the shirt. **f.** Glue hair onto the doll's head, then tie ribbon in the hair. **g.** Draw a face with a marker.

Miniature Fabric Baskets

In the true spirit of Christmas, these gifts are created with love, delivered with enthusiasm, and received with pleasure.

WHAT YOU NEED

⁵⁄₆₄" drill bit and drill (optional)

26-gauge wire

Beads (optional)

Craft batting

Desired trims for handle and top edging

Fabric

Fabric pen

Fabric scissors

Gift tag (optional)

Hot-glue gun and glue sticks

Rubber band

Small can

String

Tape measure

Tissue paper

Wire cutters

WHAT YOU DO

1. Measure the height of the can. Add 2". Place can right side up on wrong side of fabric. Making sure fabric pen is always the determined measurement away from the can, trace a circle around the can. Cut out circle.

2. Cut batting to height of the can and long enough to wrap around the can two times. Hot-glue batting to can.

3. Center can on wrong side of fabric circle. Bring the edges of the fabric to the rim of the can. Place a rubber band around the can and fabric just below the rim and adjust gathers to desired look. Trim fabric if necessary. Tie a piece of string tightly around rubber band. Hot-glue fabric close to the rim of the can.

4. For a trim handle, cut trim to desired length of handle plus 1". Glue ½" at each end of trim to the opposite sides of the can.

5. Option: For a beaded handle, cut a piece of 26-gauge wire to desired length. Drill two small holes on opposite sides of the can at the rim. Insert wire through the hole on one side, and twist the wire together a few times to secure. String beads onto the wire. Leave enough wire to place through second hole. Twist to secure.

6. Measure around the rim of the can. Cut trim to determined measurement. Hot-glue trim along the rim, covering the string, rubber bands, and ends of handles.

7. Place tissue paper inside, then fill the basket with candies or nuts.

Miniature Hatboxes

Give a little hatbox to dress up someone's desktop. It is a great place to keep rubber bands, paper clips, and thumbtacks.

WHAT YOU NEED

Adhesive gems
Buttons
Decoupage medium
Lace or ribbon
Paper flowers
Pearls
Round papier-mâché box
Lace-look scrapbook paper
Sponge brush

WHAT YOU DO

1. Rip scrapbook paper into pieces.
2. Using the sponge brush, apply decoupage medium to the box. Adhere paper onto the box. At the top of the box, fold paper over the lip to the inside of the box. Follow the same steps for the inside of the box and the box lid.
3. Apply a light coat of decoupage medium over entire box. Let dry
4. Glue lace onto the side of the lid. Decorate the top of the lid with paper flowers, buttons, pearls, and adhesive gems.

USE MULTIPURPOSE CEMENT TO ATTACH ¼" DECORATIVE JEWELS TO THE TOP OF LARGE PAPER CLIPS BEFORE ADDING THEM TO THE BOX.

Sweet Christmas Blossom

This miniature arrangement is a unique container for a chocolate lover's treat. The spirit of friendship will be sure to blossom when this sweet gift is delivered.

WHAT YOU NEED

2½" clay pot
Cellophane bag
Decoupage medium
Dried flower and greens
Floral tape
Handmade paper
Lace and/or ribbon
Small chocolate candies
Sponge brush

WHAT YOU DO

1. Rip the handmade paper into small pieces.

2. Using the sponge brush, apply decoupage medium to the surface of the clay pot. Apply paper pieces until pot is covered. Let dry.

3. Cut the flower and greens to desired length, then wrap with floral tape, covering the stem completely.

4. Place cellophane bag into the pot and fill bag with candy.

5. Insert flower and position as desired. Tie with ribbon and lace.

Memories in Miniature

Receiving photos of loved ones is always appreciated, especially when those photos are given in an exquisite album or a decorative frame. The projects on these pages range from simple to very intricate; but whichever you choose to give, the recipient will appreciate the beautiful details and the time spent.

Miniature albums and frames give you lots of possibilities. Because they are small, you can spend more time on the details and make more than one project.

Take that opportunity to experiment with different styles, colors, and themes. Use different decorative papers, interesting embellishments, and fancy ribbons and trims. Put your own spin on it. You can also personalize it for the recipient in his or her favorite colors, or design a theme with the recipient's hobbies and interests in mind.

Tin Photo Basket

*Flowers and smiling faces are sure
to warm the heart of a loved one.*

WHAT YOU NEED
Paper roses (12)
Reduced color-copied photographs
Round paper clips
Tin basket

WHAT YOU DO

1. Place the paper roses in the basket. Attach
the paper clips to the stems of roses.

2. Slide the photocopies into the paper clips.

TIP: This charming gift can be altered to create
several different looks. Replace the tin basket
with a weathered white wrought-iron basket for
a vintage look. A wicker basket and miniature lily
of the valley generates a country look. To create
a natural feel, fill a grapevine basket with sprays
of miniature red berries and evergreens.

Frames

Take inexpensive mini frames from plain to pretty, using ribbons, beads, and other embellishments.

WHAT YOU NEED

Braided trim or cord
Fabric adhesive
Miniature scrapbook frames
Various embellishments

WHAT YOU DO

1. Glue trim around frames.

2. Glue embellishments onto the ends of the trim.

GLUE MINIATURE BABY BUTTONS ONTO A SMALL WHITE FRAME FOR A DIFFERENT, YET EQUALLY PRETTY, LOOK.

Patchwork Picture Frame

This homespun patchwork frame looks darling on its own, or try hanging two or three in a row. You can make individual versions for photos of each child in the family, using different fabrics in coordinating colors.

WHAT YOU NEED

⅛"-thick x 3¼"-square
  pieces of balsa wood (2)
½"-wide ribbon
26-gauge wire
Adhesive interfacing
Gift-shaped appliqué
Beads
Broadcloth
Charms
Coordinating fabrics
  (4 pieces)
Craft knife

Fabric scissors
Hot-glue gun and
  glue sticks
Iron
Needle and
  matching thread
Photograph
Quilt batting
Rickrack
Sequins
Transparent sheet
Wire cutters
Frame pattern (page 107)

WHAT YOU DO

1. Cut out fabrics according to frame pattern. Fit pieces together like a puzzle. Iron fabric interfacing to fabric, then iron fabric to broadcloth.

2. Trace a 1¼" square in the center of the fabric. Using craft knife, cut an X from corner to corner of the square. *Note: This is where the picture will go.*

3. Stitch beads and rickrack along each seam, stopping ½" from the edge of the fabric.

4. Cut two 3¼"-square pieces from batting. Cut a 1¼" square from the center of both batting pieces.

5. Use the craft knife to cut a 1¼" square from the center of one piece of the balsa wood. Layer and hot-glue both pieces of batting onto wood.

6. Center patchwork fabric over the batting. Pull each piece of the X to the back side of the wood, then hot-glue it onto the wood. On the outsides of the frame, hot-glue the excess fabric to the back side of the wood.

7. Cut a 4½" square from broadcloth. Center the remaining piece of wood on the fabric. Fold the excess fabric over the back of wood and hot-glue to secure. This will become the back of the frame.

8. Cut two pieces of ribbon to 1½". Fold ribbon in half to form a loop. Glue ribbon to back side of the frame, placing each loop 1" in from the outside of the frame.

9. Apply hot glue down sides and bottom of the back of the frame, close to the outside edges. Leave the top unglued for inserting the photo. Adhere the back of the frame to the back of the front of the frame.

10. Hot-glue sequins as desired onto the fabric. Hot-glue the gift appliqué to the corner of the frame.

11. Cut a 2" square from the transparent sheet. Slip in through the top of frame along with the photograph.

12. To hang frame, cut a piece from wire to 7". String beads on the wire. Secure the ends of the beaded wire to the ribbon loops at the top of the frame.

Memory Book

Take the bare bones of a little book and create your own miniature scrapbook or journal.

what you need

Craft scissors

Decoupage medium

Double-sided tape

Hot-glue gun and glue sticks

Miniature book

Photograph

Quick-drying craft glue

Several sheets of coordinating scrapbook paper, enough to fill the inside of the book plus 3 sheets for the outside and inside covers

Small frame

Sponge brush

Tassel

WHAT YOU DO

1. Tear out pages from an old miniature book. Set the cover aside.

2. Measure the size of the book's pages. Take several sheets of scrapbook paper to the copy store. Have the copy store cut the paper to the determined measurement and bind it together.

3. Choose a paper for the cover of the book. Lay the cover out flat. Measure the cover from side to side and top to bottom, adding 1" all around. Cut out the paper. Apply decoupage medium to the outside of the book. Center the book on the wrong side of paper. Adhere the paper to the book, smoothing out any wrinkles. Fold the edges over to the inside of book. Secure the edges with quick-drying craft glue.

4. Hot-glue the tassel onto the top edge binding of book. Hot-glue the scrapbook pages inside the binding.

5. Measure the size of the inside pages and double the width. Cut two pieces of scrapbook paper to determined measurement. Using sponge brush, apply decoupage medium to the front inside cover and the first page. Adhere one scrapbook sheet onto the front inside cover and the first page, smoothing out any wrinkles. Repeat on the back inside cover and last page.

6. Close the book. Add weight on top of the book until decoupage medium is dry.

7. Cut photo to size of frame. Tape it onto the front of the book, using double-sided tape. Hot-glue the frame on top of the picture.

Foldout Album

This miniature scrapbook foldout album is an extra-special present for a teenager or adult when personalized to show the Christmases of his or her life. You can replace the vellum sayings with cards, stamped or written with the year the photo was taken.

WHAT YOU NEED

2"-wide ribbon (8")
12"-square vellum sheet with
   Christmas sayings
Adhesive dots
Craft scissors
Foldout album
Metal corners
Patterned paper
Quick-drying craft glue
Small leather frame with photograph
Various embellishments

WHAT YOU DO

1. Glue patterned paper onto the covers of the foldout album, making certain to miter the corners of the paper for reduced thickness.

2. Cut out different-sized sections of the vellum sheet around each saying. Place a larger section on the cover, then use adhesive dots to attach metal corners to the vellum and to the cover. (Vellum sections can also be attached with decorative brads.)

3. Tie knots at the top and bottom of the ribbon. Using adhesive dots, adhere the ribbon lengthwise to the cover, as shown in the photo to the left.

4. Attach the framed photo over the center of the ribbon with adhesive dots.

5. Using different patterned papers, photos, ribbons, vellum sections, and embellishments, decorate the inside pages.

MAKE A CONDENSED VERSION OF A MINIATURE SCRAPBOOK BY COVERING HEAVIER CARDSTOCK IN DECORATIVE PAPER. FOLD IN HALF, ADD EMBELLISHMENTS SUCH AS A TASSEL AND PRETTY PAPER TRIM, AND ADHERE PHOTOS TO THE INSIDE, USING DECORATIVE PHOTO CORNERS.

Peek-a-Boo Album

*The photo at the back of this clever album
can be seen through three "windows," squares
cut from the centers of three pieces of cardstock.
A glimpse over the top of the album reveals
a pretty design on each page.*

WHAT YOU NEED

⅛"–¼"-wide ribbon

2"-square hole punch

Brads (4)

Cardboard

Metal clasp

Patterned papers in several
    coordinating designs

Photograph

Quick-drying craft glue

Red cardstock

WHAT YOU DO

1. Cut two pieces from cardstock to 4" x 12". On both pieces, score every 1" and fold like a fan.

2. Cut four 4" x 5" pieces of cardstock. Cover each with a different patterned paper. Punch out a square from the center of three pieces.

3. Cut eight 1" x 4" strips of cardstock. Fold in half lengthwise.

4. Turn the 4" x 5" pieces over. Glue two of the folded strips onto the right and left sides of each piece, aligning the folded edge of strip with the side edge of the piece. Let glue dry.

5. To attach the 4" x 5" pieces to the accordion, glue the attached paper strips onto the inside folds of the accordion from front to back. Make certain the patterned sides of the pieces all face the same way.

6. Glue a photo onto the remaining 4" x 5" piece. Glue the piece onto the last two folds of the accordion.

7. Make presents from several different patterned papers and cardstock, ribbon, and trim. Glue them around the open windows.

8. Cut two 2½" x 4" pieces of cardboard. Cover front and back with patterned paper and trim. Glue onto front fold of accordion.

9. Using brads, attach the metal clasp to the two cardboard pieces as shown in the photo to the left.

(RIGHT) WHEN SEEN FROM THE FRONT OF THE OPEN ALBUM, THE PHOTO IS FRAMED BY "PRESENTS" MADE FROM PATTERNED PAPERS, CARDSTOCK, AND RIBBONS. **(ABOVE)** WITH DECORATIVE PAPER, TRIM, AND A GOLD CLASP GRACING THE COVER, THE ALBUM LOOKS PRETTY EVEN WHEN CLOSED.

Christmas Star Album

This remarkable project takes some time and effort, but it is well worth it. Made from folded pieces of cardstock glued back-to-back, the album can be opened 360° and tied together, revealing a red and green starburst design.

WHAT YOU NEED

¼"–½"-wide ribbon (14")

3" x 6" pieces of green cardstock (7)

3" x 7" pieces of green cardstock (7)

3¼" x 5" pieces of cardboard (2)

3" x 10" pieces of red cardstock (7)

4¼" x 6" pieces of patterned paper (2)

6½"-square pieces of double-sided plaid and
    green cardstock (7)

Christmas stickers or embellishments

Craft scissors

Hammer

Nylon-covered wire (1½ yards)

Punch tool

Quick-drying craft glue

Small beads (24)

Small clamps

Pattern for hole punch (page 108)

Pattern for album tree (page 108)

WHAT YOU DO

1. Fold pieces of red cardstock in half. This will be Layer 1.

2. Fold 3" x 6" green pieces in half. Fold these in half again to create seven 1½" x 3" pieces. This will be Layer 2.

3. Trace hole punch pattern onto cardstock. Fold it along the dotted line. Using punch tool and hammer, punch out holes.

4. Place each piece of Layer 2 inside each piece of Layer 1. (The open (non-folded) end of Layer 2 should be at the bottom.)

5. Using template on the inside, punch four holes along the spine of each nested piece (Diagram 1 on page 83).

6. Beginning inside the first nested piece, thread each end of the wire through the two center holes to the outside of the spine (Diagram 2 on page 83). Make certain the wire ends are even.

7. Cross the wire ends and thread each back through the opposite center holes to the inside of the nested pieces.

8. Thread each end of the wire through the nearest end hole to the outside of the pages (Diagram 3).

9. Place the second set of nested pages next to the first, making certain both open ends of Layer 2 are at the top. Thread the wire into the corresponding end holes of the second pages. Pull wire tightly but not hard enough to tear the cardstock.

10. Thread each wire end through the nearest center hole of the second set of pages and pull to the outside of spine. Add eight beads to one end of the wire, then thread it through the opposite center hole to the inside of the second set of pages (Diagram 4). (You will only be adding beads to the second, fourth, and sixth pages.)

11. Thread the remaining end of the wire (on the outside of the spine) through the beads as well, then thread it through the opposite center hole to the inside of the second pages.

12. Repeat Steps 9–11, adding pages and beading only the even pages until all seven have been threaded together. Note: On odd pages, when there is no beading, simply cross threads over without adding any beads. When threading is finished, tie off threads with two square knots in the center holes of inside last pages. When the book is closed, the beads should show on the spine.

13. Glue the red cardstock that is back-to-back together where they meet, making certain there is no excess glue. Hold book together with small clamps until glue is dry.

14. Glue patterned paper onto the front of the cardboard pieces. Miter corners, then fold edges over and glue onto the back side. Decorate front cover as desired.

15. Cut ribbon in half. Glue ribbon pieces onto each end of the covers. Glue covers in place on outside pieces of the book. Align covers, then close the book and place under a weight until glue is dry.

16. Fold 3" x 7" green cardstock pieces in half. Apply glue to each 3" edge and insert into each open page. Glue only the edges of the insert to the edges of each page, making certain there is no excess glue. Hold book together with clamps until glue is dry.

17. Fold double-sided cardstock pieces in half, plaid side in, to create seven 3" x 6" pieces. Trace album tree pattern on page 108 onto one side of the fold, with bottom of tree along the folded edge. Cut out. Fold each layer again so that tree is folded in half vertically. Insert one piece into each of the seven open pages, gluing just the edges to the edges of each page, making certain there is no excess glue. Hold book together with clamps until glue is dry.

18. Add stickers or embellishments to the tree and pockets. It is helpful to wrap the sides of the pages together with stickers. This will help keep photos or scrapbook pages in place.

19. Reduce and photocopy Christmas scrapbook pages or use small wallet-size photos to insert in pockets on sides of the trees.

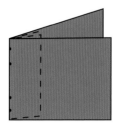

DIAGRAM 1

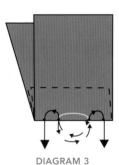

DIAGRAM 2

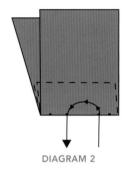

DIAGRAM 3

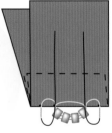

DIAGRAM 4

Christmas collections

Christmas miniatures are some of the most sought-after and popular items to collect. Perhaps it's because there is so much to choose from: nativity scenes, Santa figurines, nutcrackers, vintage toys, snow globes, music boxes, and more. It's also the fun of building an entire world from the ground up, as with a dollhouse or a village at the North Pole. Above all, it's because holiday miniatures remind us of the magic, wonder, and warmth of the season.

Collections to Create

If your Christmas decorations are lacking when it comes to groups of similar items, don't worry. You can create collections on your own whenever you want the added impact of groupings in your holiday decorating.

The trick to creating a collection is to make a variation on a theme. The variations can be whatever you like. For instance, you can paint the same wooden figurines in different colors. Or, you can purchase several figurines of the same type in different styles (such as different-looking teddy bears) and add similar embellishments.

When the elements of your collection share more than one characteristic, such as the same material and the same theme (Santa figurines all made of wood, for example), the collection will look more put together, yet will still be interesting and unique.

teddy bear collections

Teddy bears remain a favorite item to display in the home at Christmas. Perhaps it is because the teddy bear is a classic toy, and toys are such a big part of Christmas. Whatever the reason, bears are wonderfully versatile and add warmth and charm to your home.

You don't have to purchase Christmas bears to add to or start a bear collection—it's easy to turn any bear into a holiday

decoration. Place a bear in a Christmas-themed scenario—on a sleigh, under a miniature tree, or holding a present, for instance. Give the bear an activity like playing an instrument. Dress bears in cozy sweaters or fancy holiday dresses. Add bonnets, scarves, winter hats, mittens, bow ties, or stockings.

These same ideas can be applied to any figurine. Enjoy the process of creating an entire character with clothing, props, settings, and embellishments. Every year, you can put your creativity to work and enjoy making something new.

Salt Dough Bears

Create an entire collection of baked salt-dough bears, using basic ingredients from your kitchen. These decorations are fun to make with the kids—just make sure they know the bears are non-edible.

WHAT YOU NEED

4 cups flour

1 cup salt

1½ cups hot water

WHAT YOU DO

1. Preheat oven to 225°F (107°C)

2. In a large bowl, mix flour with salt. Add hot water, a little at a time, until you reach a doughy consistency.

3. Shape the dough into bears, embellish with different-colored hard candies, then bake until hardened.

4. Display the bears unadorned, or paint them with poster paints or acrylic paints. Protect them from moisture by adding a coat of lacquer or varnish.

nutcracker collections

Soldier Nutcracker

This classic nutcracker is easy to make using paint and decorative touches.

WHAT YOU NEED

#1 script liner

#6 shader

¼"-wide heavy gold ribbon (3")

Acrylic paints in black, black-green, burgundy, medium flesh, metallic gold, spice brown, and white

Blank soldier nutcracker

Hot-glue gun and glue sticks

One-sided razor blade

Pencil

Small piece of faux fur

Spray acrylic sealer

Stylus

WHAT YOU DO

1. Using the shader, paint the nutcracker as follows: body and arms with burgundy; face and hands with medium flesh; hat with black-green; shoulders with gold; legs with black; stand with spice brown. Using the liner, paint a thin stripe around the bottom of the sleeve cuffs with gold. Let paint dry.

2. Draw in the face with a pencil according to the Pattern Detail.

3. Using the liner, paint the eyes and mustache with white. Let paint dry.

4. Paint a large black dot in the center of the eyes.

5. Paint the cheeks with burgundy. Mix a small amount of white and burgundy to form pink, then dot the outside top of each cheek, using the stylus.

6. Mix a small amount of white and spice brown and add a few hair lines in the mustache.

7. Using the stylus, add random dots with gold at the top of the hat, jacket, and sleeve.

8. Spray the entire project with acrylic sealer.

9. Hot-glue the ribbon around the base of the hat.

10. Using the razor blade, cut the back side of the faux fur into small pieces for the hair and beard. Hot-glue the fur in place.

PATTERN DETAIL

Elf Nutcracker

*Create a cute elf by by painting
and adding fur to a blank nutcracker.*

WHAT YOU NEED

#1 or #2 script liner

#6 shader

Acrylic paints in baby blue, black,
   burgundy, spice brown, medium
   flesh, metallic gold, plum, and white

Blank elf nutcracker

Hot-glue gun and glue sticks

Long white faux fur

One-sided razor blade

Pencil

Spray acrylic sealer

Stylus

WHAT YOU DO

*Note: The string of bells and stars came with our
nutcracker. If you are not able to find one with those
attached, just skip the steps regarding the bells and stars.*

1. Using the shader, paint the nutcracker as follows: face and hands with medium flesh; top of the arms and torso with plum; hat (except the ball and band) and lower part of the body with burgundy; shoes with black; legs with baby blue; cuffs, band of hat, and ball at top of hat with white; stand with spice brown. Paint the string of bells and stars with gold. Let paint dry.

2. Using the pencil, lightly draw in the face, according to the Pattern Detail

3. Mix some white and burgundy, then paint in the cheeks, using the script liner.

4. Paint the entire eye, the brows, and the mustache white. Paint a light layer of spice brown on the upper eyelid. Paint the lower iris with baby blue. With black, line the upper and lower eyelids, pull out the lashes, and dot the pupil of the eye.

5. Using the stylus, add three dots of burgundy to the outside edges of the cheek circles. Then lightly line the mustache and brows with spice brown.

6. Using the stylus and white paint, make the snowflakes.

7. Using the script liner, stripe the socks with gold. Then paint black dots at random on the socks.

8. Apply three coats of acrylic sealer, allowing drying time between each.

9. Using the razor blade, cut a strip of fur to ¾" x 1½" for the beard. Cut a strip of fur to 1" x 5" for the hair. Hot-glue fur pieces into place.

10. Attach the string of bells and stars.

PATTERN DETAIL

snow people collections

Frosty Family

This handsome trio is a mini collection in itself. But if you feel inspired, use these directions as a guideline for creating a larger collection of snow people, each with its own personality.

⅛"-diameter dowel

⅛" drill bit and drill

1" flat paintbrush

3" wreath

5" doily

6" decorative trim

7" felt hat

Acrylic paints in black, burnt orange, and white

Wooden balls, 5", 6", and 7"

Band saw

Blush

Child's sock

Cotton swab

Decorative buttons, 2 for boy and 3 for father

Different-shaped balusters (3)

Embroidery floss

Hairspray

Hot-glue gun and glue sticks

Jeweled button

Moss

Sandpaper

Scrap from an old sweater

Scraps of fabric for boy's scarf and band of father's hat

Sewing machine and matching thread

Small berries

Small paintbrush

Ultrafine glitter

Wood glue

WHAT YOU DO

1. Using band saw, cut the balusters to 6", 8", and 9". Using wood glue, adhere flat part of wooden ball to cut part of baluster. Let dry overnight.

2. Paint the entire body of all three snow people white. Let paint dry. Sand snow people for a weathered look.

3. Using ⅛" drill bit, drill holes in all three balls where nose belongs. Cut one piece from dowel to ¼" and two pieces to ½". Sand each to a point, then paint with burnt orange paint. Let paint dry.

4. Using a dab of wood glue, insert the noses into the holes.

5. To decorate the boy, cut off the top of the sock, then cut a fringe 1" long around one end. Tie in the middle with embroidery floss. Place unfringed end on the head. Turn up ½" to make a cuff. Lift hat and hot-glue it onto the head. Cut a scrap from fabric to 1" x 9". Fringe both ends. Tie it around the neck. Hot-glue two decorative buttons onto the front of the boy.

6. To decorate the mother, cut a slit in the center of the doily. Place around the mother's neck and secure with hot glue. Hot-glue 6" decorative trim around the neck. Hot-glue jeweled button onto the center front of trim. Hot-glue the wreath around the top of the head. Hot-glue moss and berries in desired arrangement.

7. To decorate the father, cut a 2" x 18" scarf from an old piece of sweater. Fold scarf in half lengthwise and sew together. Turn right side out. Fringe both ends of scarf. Tie it around the neck. Hot-glue three buttons down the front. Hot-glue the felt hat to the head, then hot-glue moss and berries onto the hat in desired arrangement.

8. Spray each snow person with hairspray. Sprinkle with ultrafine glitter before the hairspray dries. Using the opposite end of the small paintbrush, dot in black paint for eyes and mouth. Using a cotton swab, apply blush to the cheeks.

Snow Angel

Enjoy the charm this lovely lady brings to your holiday decor.

WHAT YOU NEED

⅛"-diameter dowel

1½"-wide wire-edged ribbon (12")

3" straw hat

5" doily

Acrylic paints in black, burnt orange, and white

Berries, moss, and preserved pine

Blush

Buttons (3)

Cotton swab

Craft scissors

Crochet thread

Fabric scissors

Funnel

Hot-glue gun and glue sticks

Kitty litter or sand (¾ cup)

Muslin (¼ yard)

Needle and matching thread

Palette

Polyester stuffing

Sandpaper

Sewing machine and matching thread

Small paintbrush

Tiny bird's nest and bird

Twigs

Washed sand (⅛ cup)

Pattern (page 108)

WHAT YOU DO

1. Trace snow angel pattern on a doubled piece of muslin. Cut out both pieces.

2. Sew pieces together. Make a slit in the neck on the back layer of muslin. Turn right side out. Using a funnel, fill the bottom with kitty litter. Stuff the remainder of body with polyester stuffing until it is firm. Stitch slit closed.

3. Mix the washed sand with white paint to desired thickness and texture. Cover the entire body with the mixture.

4. Using the handle end of the paintbrush, dot eyes on face with black paint. Using a cotton swab, apply blush to the cheeks. For the nose, cut the dowel ¾" long with scissors, then sand the end to a point with sandpaper. Paint the nose with orange. Make a small hole just under the eyes for the nose. Insert the dowel into the hole.

5. Tie ribbon around neck for the scarf. Hot-glue three buttons down the front.

6. Make small slits for arms. Insert twigs and secure them with hot glue. Hot-glue nest, bird, and moss onto sticks.

7. Hot-glue hat onto head, then decorate with berries, moss, and preserved pine.

8. Gather doily in the center with crochet thread, then tie in a knot to create the shape of wings. Hot-glue to the back of Snow Angel.

Miniature Christmas Villages

This is the time of year when adults get to play, too, and many of us exercise our imaginations by setting up miniature Christmas villages in our homes. Indulge in this collecting craze with caution: what starts with a quaint ceramic church and perhaps a cottage or two, often grows into an entire town that threatens to take up every inch of space in your home.

Tabletops, sideboards, and even countertops can all be turned into winter wonderlands. If space is at a premium, a round, tiered shelf can make a lovely multi-level display. Villages come with lights, sounds, and even movement. Snow, available in various forms is a must.

Whether your village is urban or rural, peopled with Victorian figures or populated with playful animal figurines, its effect can be magical. Children love gazing at the scene, imagining themselves skating on the little ice pond or walking into the tiny candy shop, and adult guests will be eager to see each year's newest additions.

Displaying Collections

Creating chic holiday decor in your home doesn't have to be complicated. In fact, it's as easy as combining groups of similar miniatures you've collected over the years. Whether you tend to accumulate carved wooden Santas, tin soldiers, or ceramic animals, simply place them together on a table or mantel, add touches like greenery or garlands, and you have a nearly effortless holiday display.

Collections—especially ones that have been handed down and added to through the years—bring back a sense of warmth and nostalgia from Christmases past. Make room for your collections every year, and they will become part of the familiar surroundings that make up what Christmas means to you.

Setting the Scene

When displaying a collection, consider the setting first. A collection as large as a Christmas village needs room and can be the focal point in your Christmas decorations. Give worthy collections a place of honor and rearrange other items to accommodate them. Collections that are large can be displayed more impressively by using different levels. I like to use antique wooden boxes, or pots and goblets turned upside down. Other items can be used as well and covered with tablecloths, placemats, or fabric.

Small miniature collections can be incorporated in a dining-room table centerpiece, in front of the fireplace, on the mantel, or even on a windowsill.

One of my favorite spots for my nativity is under the grand piano. I like to divide my Santa collection and place the figurines in different rooms all over the house.

"Christmas — that magic blanket that wraps itself about us, that something so intangible that it is like a fragrance. It may weave a spell of nostalgia. Christmas may be a day of feasting, or of prayer, but always it will be a day of remembrance — a day in which we think of everything we have ever loved."

~Augusta E. Rundel

Using Bookcases

Consider removing some of your everyday items during December and replacing them with Christmas decor.

Wooden bookcases are a wonderful place for collections. You can create all kinds of backgrounds to enhance the display. Hang glittered fabric, paper, or holiday prints on the shelf back to embellish and suit the style of the collection. For a special touch, hang lights or paper icicles across the top.

Wooden stars, covered in fabric, decorative paper, and glitter add extra glam to a collection of vintage cottages and bottle-brush trees. Try delicate lacy fabric for an ethereal touch to a collection of angels, or dark navy dotted with silver stars for a group of nativity figurines.

"[Christmas] comes every year and will go on forever. And along with Christmas belong the keepsakes and the customs. Those humble, everyday things a mother clings to, and ponders, like Mary in the secret spaces of her heart."

~Marjorie Holmes

Patterns

CARD TREE PATTERN
Pattern shown actual size

WHOLE MITTEN PATTERN
Patterns shown actual size

MITTEN TOP PATTERN

CUFF PATTERN

CONE PATTERN
Pattern shown actual size

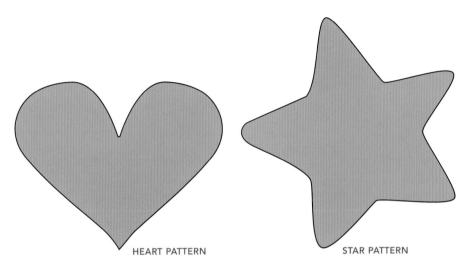

HEART PATTERN

STAR PATTERN

Patterns shown actual size

FELT STOCKING PATTERN
Enlarge pattern 200%

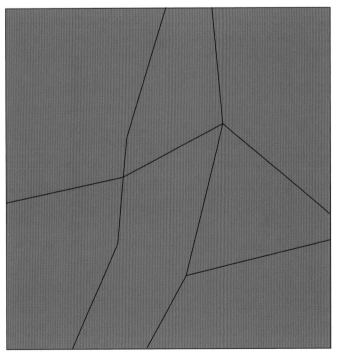

FRAME PATTERN
Enlarge pattern 200%

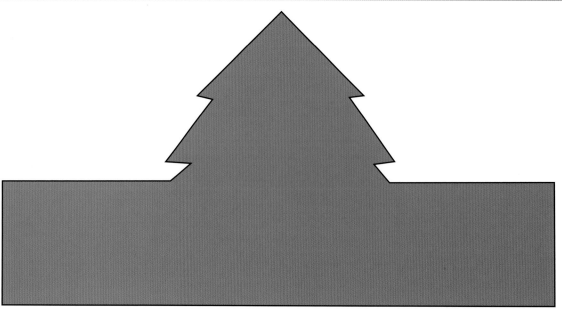

CHRISTMAS STAR ALBUM TREE PATTERN
Pattern shown actual size

**CHRISTMAS STAR ALBUM
HOLE PUNCH PATTERN**
Pattern shown actual size

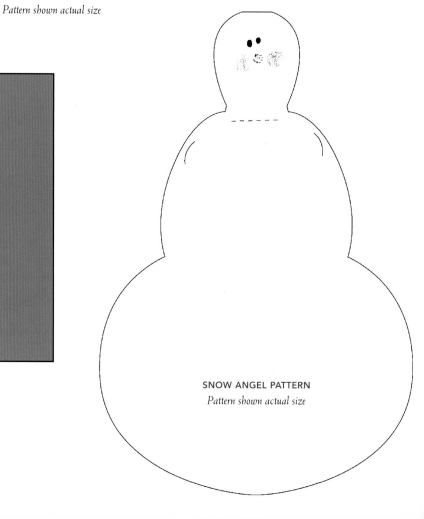

SNOW ANGEL PATTERN
Pattern shown actual size

About the Author
Diana Dunkley

Diana Dunkley is the author of *Two-Hour NoSew Decorating* and has designed for several other Chapelle books as well as *McCalls* magazine. Diana recently opened Rustic Diamond, an import, gift, and antique shop in downtown Ogden, Utah. She is a working actress, director, and costume designer with a B.A. in Theater Arts. She recently appeared in the movie *Charly* and currently works at the Desert Star Theater in Salt Lake City. She resides with her supportive husband Ralph and their family in Pleasant View, Utah. She would like to thank JoAnn, Laurie, Lisa, Chapelle, and especially Jo.

Contributors
Laurie Thompson

Laurie Thompson is happy to be designing for *A Merry Little Christmas*. Her interest in design started at an early age. Many of her creations were shared with her family, relatives, and friends as she was growing up. Today, she is still known for her creative and unique gifts and enjoys the title of "Party Queen." Laurie has designed restaurants, cabinet showrooms, and weddings in California, Nevada, and Utah. She lives in Pleasant View, Utah, where she works with her husband Dave at Anatra Cabinets. She would like to give special thanks to her husband as well as Kari, Kristin, Hailee, Colette, and Diana.

JoAnn Colledge

JoAnn Colledge is excited to add her creative designs to *A Merry Little Christmas*. A professional designer and scrapbooker, JoAnn has always had a passion for creating. Her motto is "Presentation Is Everything," and she believes things should "happen quickly, but beautifully." She lives in North Ogden, Utah, with her beautiful family and wonderful husband Ken.

Photo Credits

Reprinted by permission of Hearst Communications, Inc.: pages 35, 48 and 49
Toshi Otsuki: pages 11, 26, 28–35
Michael Skott ©1993: pages 11, 27, 30 and 31

Metric Equivalency Chart

inches to millimeters and centimeters

INCHES	MM	CM	INCHES	CM	INCHES	CM
⅛	3	0.3	9	22.9	30	76.2
¼	6	0.6	10	25.4	31	78.7
½	13	1.3	12	30.5	33	83.8
⅝	16	1.6	13	33.0	34	86.4
¾	19	1.9	14	35.6	35	88.9
⅞	22	2.2	15	38.1	36	91.4
1	25	2.5	16	40.6	37	94.0
1¼	32	3.2	17	43.2	38	96.5
1½	38	3.8	18	45.7	39	99.1
1¾	44	4.4	19	48.3	40	101.6
2	51	5.1	20	50.8	41	104.1
2½	64	6.4	21	53.3	42	106.7
3	76	7.6	22	55.9	43	109.2
3½	89	8.9	23	58.4	44	111.8
4	102	10.2	24	61.0	45	114.3
4½	114	11.4	25	63.5	46	116.8
5	127	12.7	26	66.0	47	119.4
6	152	15.2	27	68.6	48	121.9
7	178	17.8	28	71.1	49	124.5
8	203	20.3	29	73.7	50	127.0

yards to meters

YARDS	METERS	YARDS	METERS	YARDS	METERS	YARDS	METERS	YARDS	METERS
⅛	0.11	2⅛	1.94	4⅛	3.77	6⅛	5.60	8⅛	7.43
⅛	0.11	2⅛	1.94	4⅛	3.77	6⅛	5.60	8⅛	7.43
¼	0.23	2¼	2.06	4¼	3.89	6¼	5.72	8¼	7.54
⅜	0.34	2⅜	2.17	4⅜	4.00	6⅜	5.83	8⅜	7.66
⅝	0.46	2½	2.29	4½	4.11	6½	5.94	8½	7.77
⅝	0.57	2⅝	2.40	4⅝	4.23	6⅝	6.06	8⅝	7.89
¾	0.69	2¾	2.51	4¾	4.34	6¾	6.17	8¾	8.00
⅞	0.80	2⅞	2.63	4⅞	4.46	6⅞	6.29	8⅞	8.12
1	0.91	3	2.74	5	4.57	7	6.40	9	8.23
1¼	1.03	3¼	2.86	5⅛	4.69	7¼	6.52	9⅛	8.34
1¼	1.14	3¼	2.97	5¼	4.80	7¼	6.63	9¼	8.46
1⅜	1.26	3⅜	3.09	5⅜	4.91	7⅜	6.74	9⅜	8.57
1½	1.37	3½	3.20	5½	5.03	7½	6.86	9½	8.69
1⅝	1.49	3⅝	3.31	5⅝	5.14	7⅝	6.97	9⅝	8.80
1¾	1.60	3¾	3.43	5¾	5.26	7¾	7.09	9¾	8.92
1⅞	1.71	3⅞	3.54	5⅞	5.37	7⅞	7.20	9⅞	9.03
2	1.83	4	3.66	6	5.49	8	7.32	10	9.14

Index